The Crusty Ones

A First Look at Crustaceans

BY SOLVEIG PAULSON RUSSELL

DRAWINGS BY LAWRENCE DI FIORI

HENRY Z. WALCK, INC.   NEW YORK

Library of Congress Cataloging in Publication Data
Russell, Solveig Paulson,
    The crusty ones.
    SUMMARY: Surveys the class of animals called crusta-
ceans describing their characteristics, habitats,
structure, development, and importance in the food cycle.
    1. Crustacea—Juvenile literature. [1. Crustacea]
I. Di Fiori, Lawrence, illus. II. Title.
QL437.2.R87   595'.3   74-6028
ISBN 0-8098-1226-6

To Susy Clark
who loves to read about many things

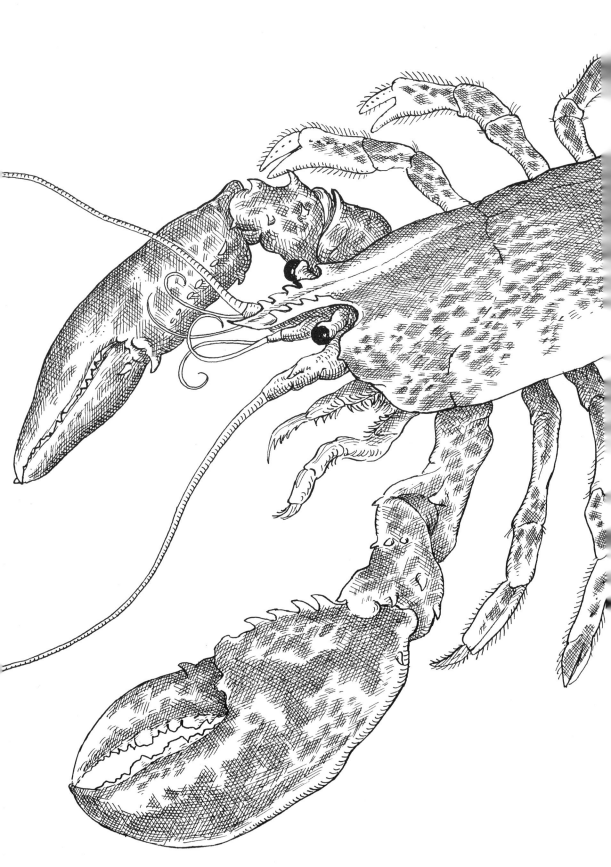

THE CRUSTY ONES are the thousands of different creatures—crabs, lobsters, crayfish, shrimp, and all their many strange relatives—that make up the class of animals called Crustacea.

The name Crustacea comes from a Latin word that means shell. Even though crustaceans don't all have shells, it's a good name for these creatures. They all do have an outer covering of a horny material called chitin that is shell-like or crusty. In some crustaceans, like the crab or lobster, the covering is hard and thick. But in others, like a few of the water fleas, it may be thin and easily bent.

There are more than twenty thousand kinds of animals that are crustaceans. Some have not even been given names. And there are such great differences among these many creatures, that it is hard to make a simple definition of them.

Crustaceans belong to a large group of animals that scientists call Arthropoda—animals with jointed feet. Crustaceans all have jointed legs, and a covering of chitin, but otherwise they don't seem to have any one common characteristic.

Perhaps as good a definition as any would be that of a scientist, T.R.R. Stebbing, who says that crustaceans have bodies made of different segments; with legs at some time in their lives; that breathe in water either through gills, or through their skins; that have no neck or wings; and that when first born move about freely in water.

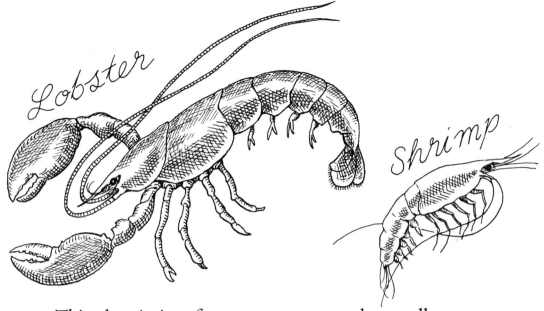

This description fits crustaceans people usually know—the crabs, shrimp and lobsters, and even barnacles that move about freely when first born. And it also fits water fleas and hermit crabs, and some creatures of cellars and gardens—the sow bugs, or pill bugs—that are less well-known crustaceans.

Crustaceans can be so small they are hard to see, and others are so large and strong that a pinch from their sharp claws can make a person yowl with pain.

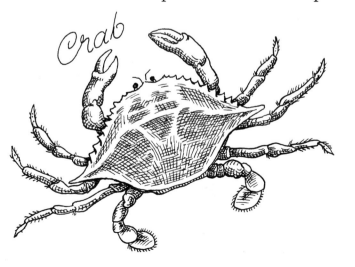

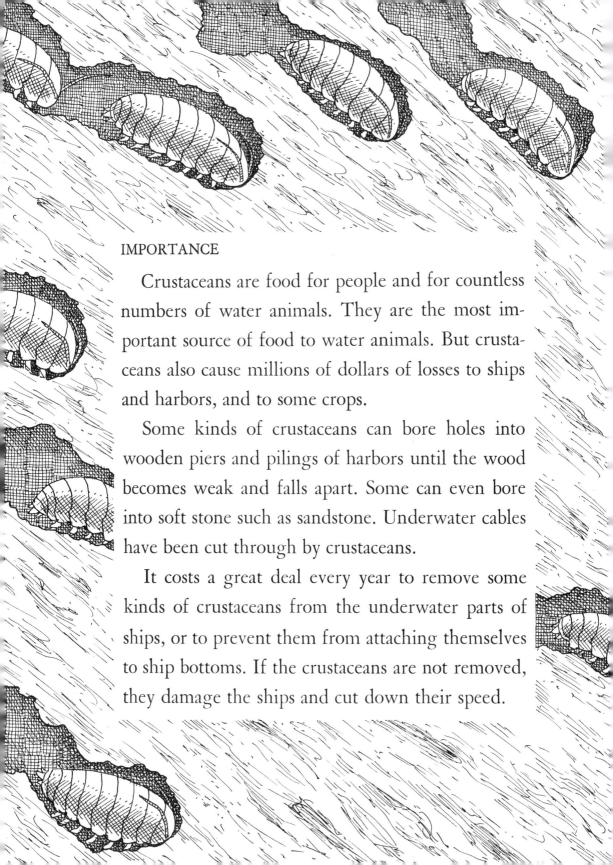

IMPORTANCE

Crustaceans are food for people and for countless numbers of water animals. They are the most important source of food to water animals. But crustaceans also cause millions of dollars of losses to ships and harbors, and to some crops.

Some kinds of crustaceans can bore holes into wooden piers and pilings of harbors until the wood becomes weak and falls apart. Some can even bore into soft stone such as sandstone. Underwater cables have been cut through by crustaceans.

It costs a great deal every year to remove some kinds of crustaceans from the underwater parts of ships, or to prevent them from attaching themselves to ship bottoms. If the crustaceans are not removed, they damage the ships and cut down their speed.

The enormous numbers and varieties of crustaceans and their importance make them interesting, yet many people know very little about these amazing creatures. We do know some things about crabs, lobsters, shrimp, crayfish and barnacles, but not much about such crustaceans as beach fleas and sea spiders. And there are other small creatures that are so different from the crustaceans people know best, that they bewilder those who try to study them.

Among these are very small crustaceans that feed on invisibly tiny bits of plants at sea. These little creatures are in turn eaten by fish and other animals. The blue whales, the world's largest living animals, feed chiefly on small crustaceans in the sea. When we think of how many billions of crustaceans these mammoth creatures must gulp down in a single day, we can get an idea of the vast numbers of tiny crustaceans that live in the sea. Without these tremendous numbers, fish and other animals of the ocean would not live.

CRUSTACEANS IN HISTORY

Crustaceans have been known to people long before any records were kept. The Babylonians, as far back as 2100 B.C., called a grouping of stars by their name for crab. This meant "workman-of-the-river-bed." The crab they knew, and ate, was a common one that lives in fresh water and burrows into swamps and stream banks.

Many centuries later the Romans called the crab by their Latin name of *Cancer*. Now we call the star group, or constellation, Cancer.

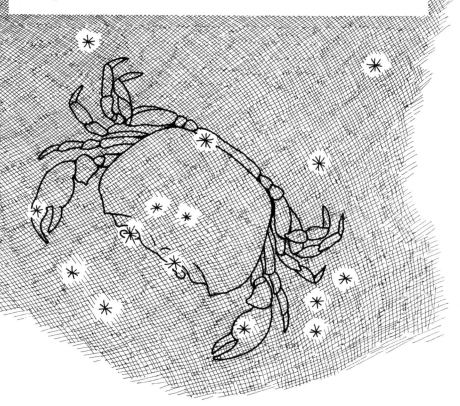

One way we know that ancient people knew about crabs and other crustaceans is that there are pictures of them on their coins. Some of these coins can still be seen in museums today.

Other pictures of crustaceans have been found in caves and on walls of old temples. Queen Hatshepsut of Egypt, who lived about three thousand years ago, had pictures in her temple showing different fish and crustaceans. Parts of other old picture records have been found also.

Aristotle, an ancient Greek philosopher, was the first known person to study crustaceans. Over two thousand years ago he identified a dozen or more species. But for about the next two thousand years, only a few people spent any time studying them. Then in the eighteenth century, Carolus Linnaeus became interested in the scientific study of plants and animals, and he learned much about crustaceans. His work was the beginning of our present study and knowledge about them.

HOW OUR BEST-KNOWN CRUSTACEANS ARE MADE

The most familiar of the crustaceans are the ones people eat—the crabs, lobsters and shrimp. These all belong to the order, or group, called Decapoda, or ten-footed ones.

Because of the great numbers and differences in all crustaceans, it is not possible here to describe how each is made. But we can look at the familiar decapods. Their bodies are made up of a number of sections, or segments. Sometimes these are joined to others, sometimes each is separate. In shrimp, lobsters and crabs the sections can be easily seen.

The sections are all covered by chitin. Some parts of the cover are thick and hard because of deposits of lime that come from the food the animals eat. Where the body is jointed, the cover is soft and thin so the joints can move.

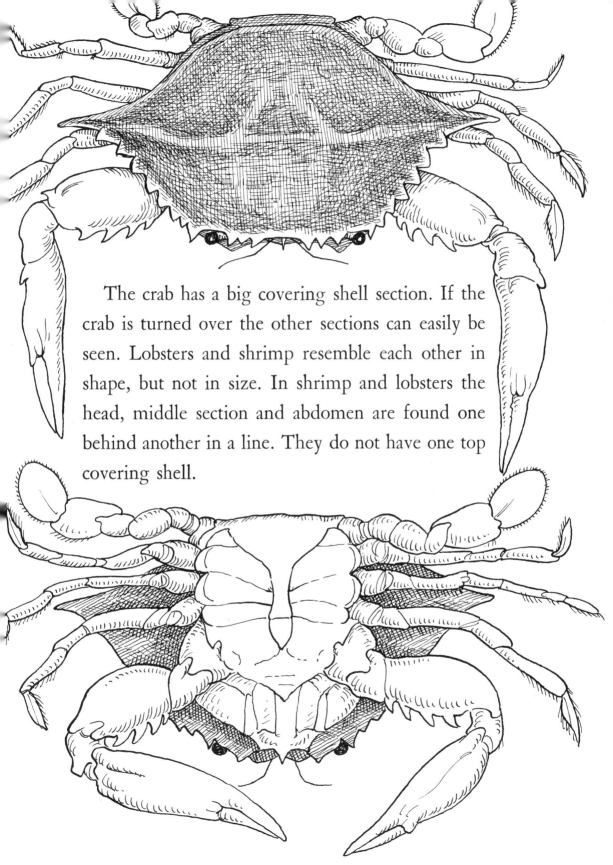

The crab has a big covering shell section. If the crab is turned over the other sections can easily be seen. Lobsters and shrimp resemble each other in shape, but not in size. In shrimp and lobsters the head, middle section and abdomen are found one behind another in a line. They do not have one top covering shell.

Attached to the decapod's main body sections are eyes, two pairs of feelers, five pairs of jointed legs, and a tail piece that folds under the end of the body and is often called an abdomen. With these parts decapods can get food, travel, fight, swim or burrow, as the need may be. If a leg is lost in a fight, or some other way, another can grow in its place. But only legs can be replaced by new growth.

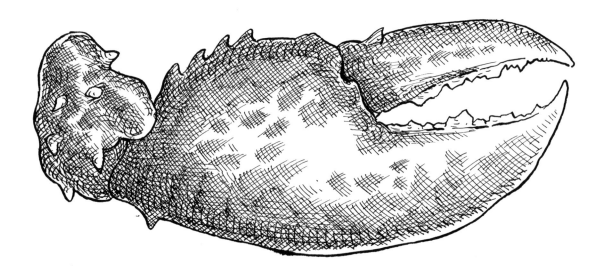

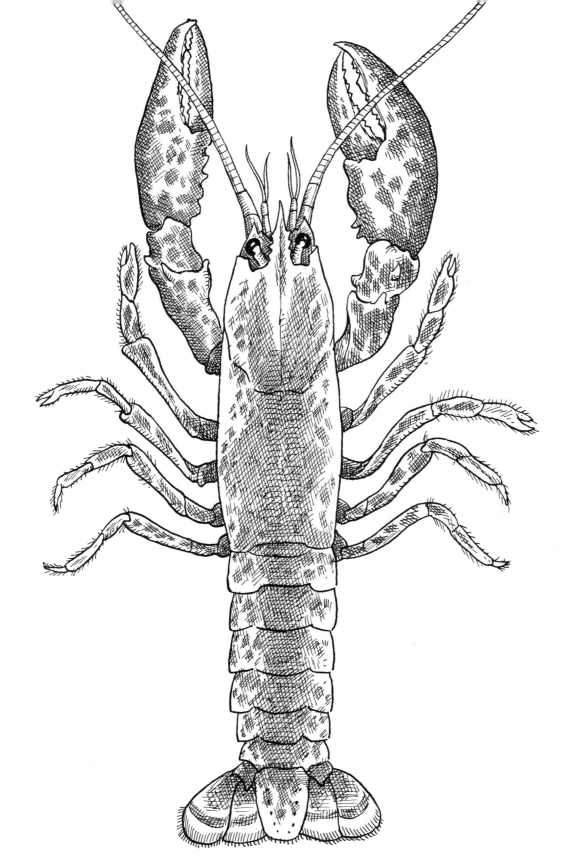

Chitin, the outside covering, forms a kind of case which protects the crustacean's body. The covering doesn't grow or stretch. So from time to time as a crustacean grows older, it needs to discard its shell for a bigger one. This is called molting. When a crab molts, a slit or crack opens at the back part of the shell and the crab crawls out, hind part first.

The new covering material which has formed under the old shell is soft, so it can expand when the old coat is off. After getting out of the old shell the crustacean swells its body by taking in water. The new coat dries and hardens to a bigger size, leaving room for inner growth within a day or so. Most crustaceans molt many times when they are young. Older ones do not need new coverings very often for they do not grow as quickly.

With many of the decapods, the female carries the eggs until they hatch. The eggs are fastened to the female's back underparts. At hatching time, the fiddler crab goes to the water's edge and fans its abdomen back and forth. With each swish the offspring break from the eggs and are sprayed forward into the water. Most other decapods launch their young in a similar way.

The baby crustaceans are a strange lot. Most do not look anything like their parents, although young crayfish, freshwater crabs and lobsters do resemble their parents. The young crustaceans go through many stages and shapes. At first they move about freely in water, eating tiny plants and animals. At this stage they may be wormlike, transparent, fringed, or follow many other growth patterns, depending upon the kind of crustacean they are. When they are ready to become adults, they sink to the water bottom. Only one in a great number escapes

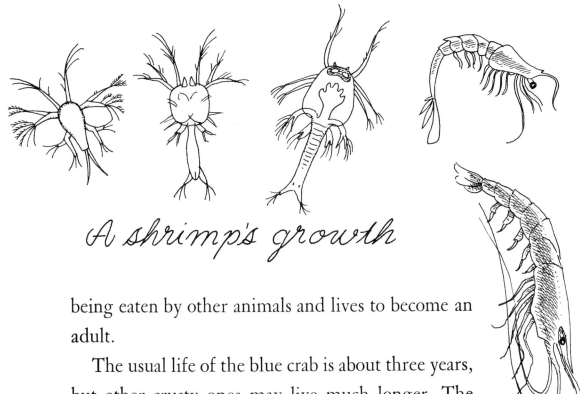

A shrimp's growth

being eaten by other animals and lives to become an adult.

The usual life of the blue crab is about three years, but other crusty ones may live much longer. The Northern lobster may live as much as fifty years, and weigh thirty or more pounds. When full-grown, these crustaceans may have bodies two feet long and claws that can reach twenty inches.

The largest crustaceans are the Giant Spider Crabs of Japan and the Northern Pacific Ocean. They measure a foot and a half across the body, and have long arms and huge pincers. The largest freshwater crayfish is about two feet long and weighs eight or nine pounds. These are found in Tasmania.

THE BEST-KNOWN CRUSTY ONES

Most of the best-known crusty ones are decapods. This group, or order, has two major divisions—the swimmers such as shrimp, and the crawlers such as lobsters and crabs. The well-known barnacles, however, are not decapods. They belong to the group called Cirripedia, or feathery-footed.

Barnacles

Anyone who has been to the ocean shore is almost sure to have seen barnacles fastened to rocks or piling. For many years it was not known that barnacles are crustaceans. They were thought to be the same kind of animal as clams, oysters, snails or mussels, which are mollusks.

Barnacles look like crusty bumps that never move. They cannot move when they are adult. But when they are first hatched, they move freely in water, like all crustaceans. After going through a number of molts and changing forms, the tiny barnacles are ready to become adults. They settle on a rock, a piece of wood, a boat, or even a seashell of some kind. Some kinds of barnacles settle on whales. There they fasten themselves for life, with a cement from glands within their bodies.

The barnacles rest with their heads down and grow a hard crusty covering about themselves. These coverings, or shells, can open enough to let the barnacles put out feathery legs into the water. The legs wave about and find tiny bits of food which they kick back into the barnacle shells. When barnacles live where low tides leave them high and dry for a while, their shells close, holding enough sea water within to keep the creatures wet and alive for some time.

As with all the crusty ones, barnacles molt as they grow. But barnacle bodies molt inside their shells. The shells are constantly enlarged by new shell material that is added to the edges.

There are many varieties of barnacles. The most common are the acorn barnacles. They look something like acorns or tiny volcanoes. Another kind is the gooseneck barnacle. It is similar to the acorn barnacle but grows on a rubbery stalk called a gooseneck.

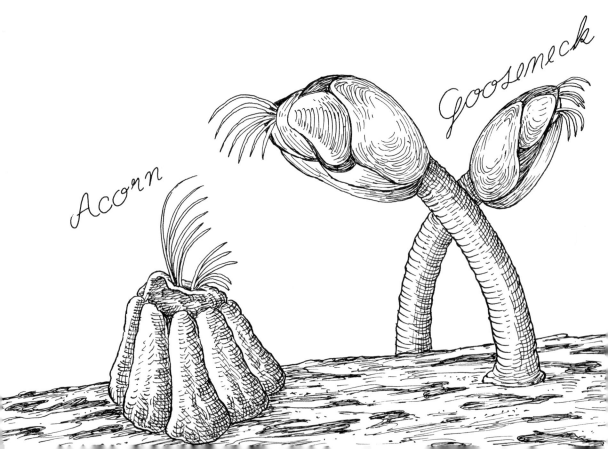

Barnacles are sometimes used as food. In Chile, one large kind is an important food. It tastes like shrimp and is used in soups and chowder. In Japan a small kind is used to make fertilizer, or plant food.

When large numbers of barnacles attach themselves to the bottom of a ship they slow the ship's speed and lengthen the time for a voyage. It costs a lot of money to keep a large ship free of barnacles and other sea creatures. In other times the bottoms had to be scraped clean, but now ships can be coated with chemical materials that repel barnacles. But even with these new methods, the life habits of barnacles are expensive for the shipping business.

Shrimp

Shrimp are considered delicious eating by people all over the world. Many millions of pounds are caught each year for food. They come mostly from the sea, but there are also freshwater shrimp. At the sea smaller shrimp live in tide pools and shallow water, and larger ones live in deeper water. Large shrimp are often called prawns.

The shrimp we usually see in markets are only the abdomen and tail. Other parts of the body have been removed. The whole shrimp looks very much like a small lobster without the lobster's big claws. Shrimp have very long feelers—almost twice as long as their bodies.

Shrimp appear in several colors–gray, greenish-blue, pink, sand-colored—and some are almost color-less. Some live in northern waters, but most live where the waters are not too cold.

Shrimp hide in sand for protection. They dig themselves down quickly and then use their long feelers to cover themselves with loose sand.

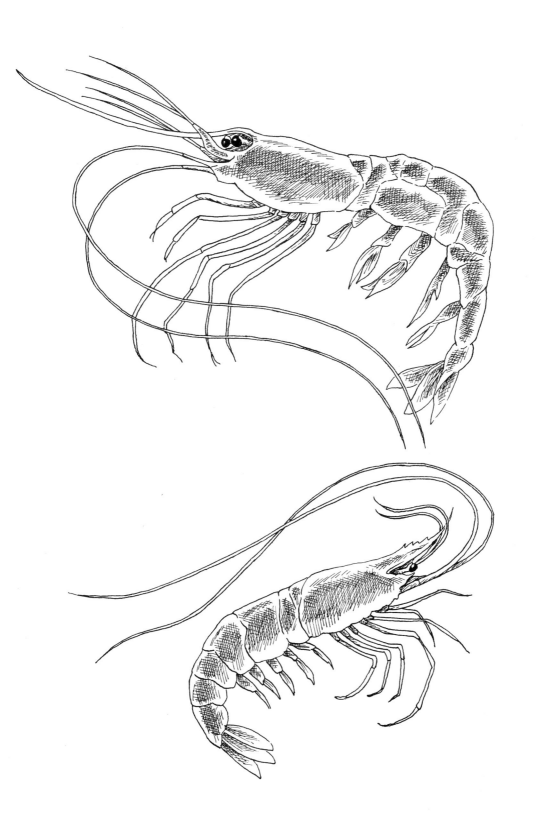

Lobsters

Lobsters, like shrimp, have long feelers with which to locate food. They have two large claws, or pincers, but these are not alike. The right one is larger and is used to crush clams or snail shells, or any other food the lobster wants to break apart. The left claw is smaller and sharper. It is used to tear food apart and to carry the food to the lobster's mouth.

When lobsters are first hatched their claws are only half as long as their bodies, but as the lobster body grows the claws grow at a much faster rate. The claws of adult lobsters are so large that they may weigh much more than the rest of the body. Sometimes they are almost too heavy for the lobster to lift. Much of the meat people eat comes from the big claws.

Lobsters live on the ocean bottom. They move about there looking for any kind of food, and they eat almost anything—even each other. They can move forward or backward, but not sideways. When moving backward a lobster spreads the flat plates at the end of the abdomen and uses them like an oar.

Lobsters are usually green, tinged with other colors, but when they have been cooked the shell turns red.

Most lobsters caught for food are a foot or more long. If a fisherman catches smaller ones in his lobster traps, he puts them back into the water to grow bigger. However there are different kinds of lobsters, of different sizes, which are caught for food. One small kind, called a chicken lobster, weighs about a pound.

It is not known which of the crusty ones lives longest, but perhaps lobsters do. In 1956 a record-breaking Northern lobster that weighed forty-four and a half pounds was caught off the coast of Long Island. It was thought to be about fifty years old.

Crayfish

Crayfish are small relatives of lobsters, and they look like them. They live in fresh water where they dig burrows, or tunnels, in the mud banks.

Like lobsters and other decapods, crayfish have five pairs of legs. The front ones are used for catching and holding small fish or other creatures which they eat.

Crayfish are usually from three to five inches long. They can walk in any direction or swim. If they are startled they seem to scoot backward very quickly.

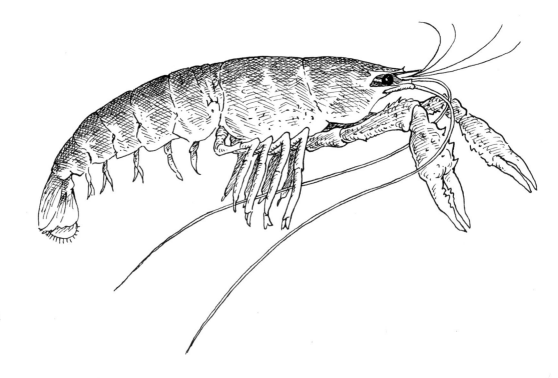

Long ago in the time of the Roman Empire crayfish were used extensively for food. Those that were meant for food for the rich were often kept in earthen jars and fed until they were fattened. Poorer people ate them as they were first caught and cooked.

Snakes, racoons, otters, alligators and some birds and other animals catch crayfish from streams for food. People both in our country and abroad also like to eat crayfish. Many thousands of pounds are caught each year. In parts of our country where there are many crayfish, children often like to wade in shallow streams to see how many crayfish they can catch.

Crabs

There are many kinds of crabs in both the Atlantic and Pacific oceans. There are blue crabs, green, calico, lady, spider, kelp, ghost, fiddler and hermit crabs—to name some. They can be seen scurrying about in tide pools and on the sand at many beaches. They hide under weeds or rocks, and dig into the sand.

Crab bodies are short and stubby in contrast to the long bodies of lobsters. They have short feelers. Most do not move backwards and forwards, but sideways. This is because their short bodies are pushed with four legs on one side and pulled with four legs on the other side.

The blue crab is the one commonly caught for food on the Atlantic Coast and in the Gulf of Mexico. It has a shell five or six inches wide and is dark green, blue or reddish in color. Great numbers are caught each year.

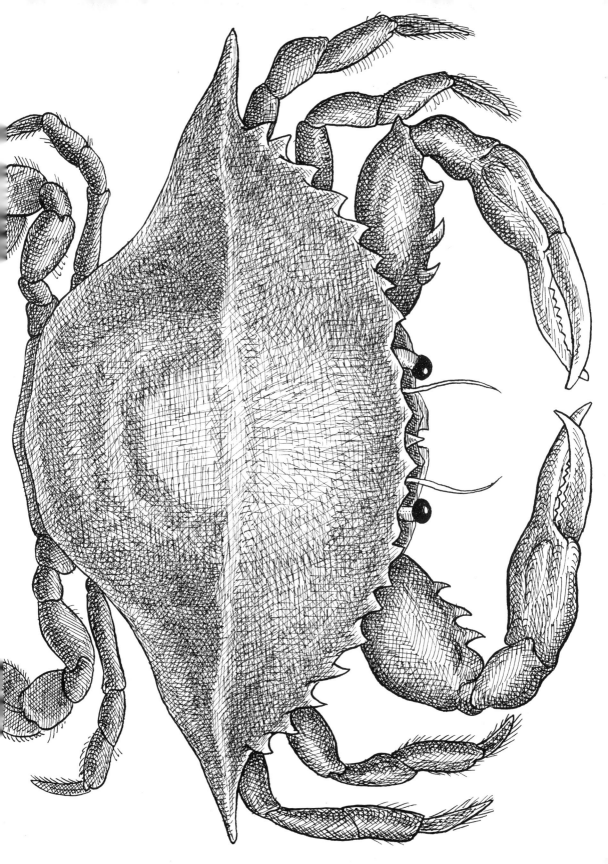

The fiddler crab gets its name because one claw of the males is much bigger than the other, and looks  something like a fiddle or violin. The smaller claw can be thought of as a bow for the violin. Male fiddlers wave their big fiddle about, especially when they want to attract females. The females have two small claws.

Fiddlers are diggers. They make long slanted tunnels in sand or mud with the entrance just below high-tide level. Before high tide they close the entrance with little balls of sand or mud so that the tunnel will not be flooded.

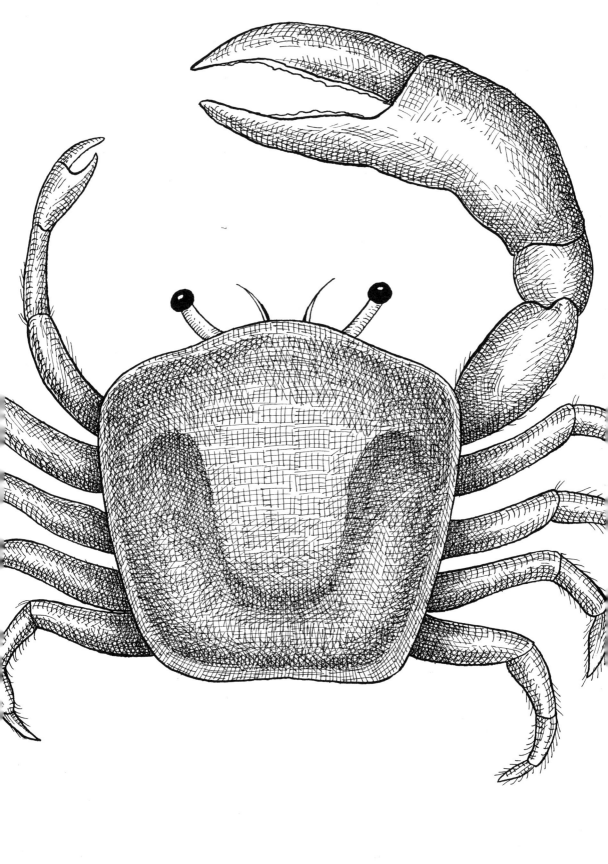

Another crab that tunnels into sandy beaches or marshes is the ghost, or sand crab, about one and a half inches wide and light in color. It moves sideways and stops and starts so quickly that anyone looking at it has trouble seeing the movements, and so it seems that the crab disappears like a ghost.

Hermit crabs are fun to watch. Their rear parts are soft and unprotected because they have no hard shell there. Hermit crabs take care of this matter by simply backing into any empty shell on the beach that fits them. With the borrowed covering of some other creature they go scurrying about, seeming perfectly comfortable. When they grow too large for the shell, they find a bigger one and back into it.

Not all crabs live in sea water. Some are fresh-water creatures. They burrow into river mud. As we have said, the old name that the Babylonians used for these crabs meant "workman-of-the-river-bed." Freshwater crabs were eaten by ancient people and in some foreign countries they are still used as food.

One interesting crab that lives in the South Seas is called the robber, or coconut crab. It climbs coconut palm trees and eats the nuts. It can easily climb over coral blocks and rough land, up trees and the doorways of houses. It has very sharp claws that fit into tiny crevices to help it climb. When ready to come down it backs downward.

During the night the robber crab makes its way up the palm trees and drills out the eye of a nut to make a hole. Then, with one of its smaller legs it scrapes out the nut meat and eats it. A robber crab can eat about two coconuts in three days. These crabs are about eighteen inches long, and have strong claws. No other animal seems to have the strength or ability to open coconuts.

The robber crab usually stays close to shore, and spends the day hiding in crevices of coral reefs, or in other safe places. When it comes out at night, people armed with torches and other lights hunt it for its delicious meat. Because of this robber crabs are becoming scarce, and may disappear unless something is done to save them.

Although these strange crusty ones live most of their lives on land they do go to the sea to lay their eggs.

CRUSTACEANS MOST PEOPLE DON'T KNOW

So far we have been generally speaking of the large order of crusty ones called the decapods, with which we are most familiar. There are other groups that differ in the number of body parts, in structure, and in other ways. These groups include creatures ranging from those who live thousands of feet above sea level, to others living as much as six hundred fathoms down in the sea.

One newly discovered kind of crustacean is a blind colorless one that lives in waters that have muddy bottoms. The largest members of this kind are about fifteen one-hundredths of an inch long. It would take about a dozen or more lined up to measure one inch. These grub-like creatures find food in mud and silt, in bays and shallow waters. Their scientific name is Cephalocarida.

Another crustacean is the brine shrimp that lives in salty water. It is one of the crustacean group called branchiopods, or gill-footed. Sometimes in salty

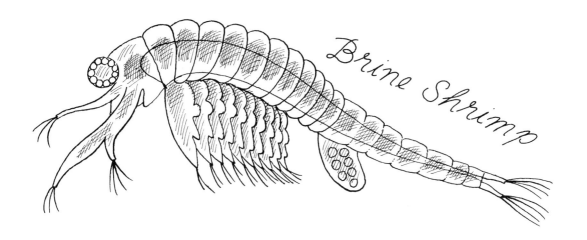

Brine Shrimp

water, such as that of Great Salt Lake in Utah, there are so many that they make the water look red or brownish-red. The color comes from the food they eat—green algae, which seems to turn red in the brine shrimp as it is digested.

"Water fleas" are tiny branchiopods that furnish most of the food for fish in the Great Lakes, although some of them are so small a microscope is needed to study them. They are called water fleas because of their jumping movements. A few have no shells, only a thin chitin covering.

Water Flea

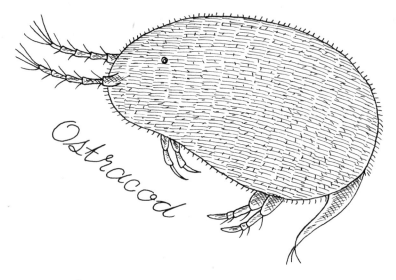

Ostracod

Another group, the ostracods, are crustaceans that live in all kinds of water—even roadside puddles. These are enclosed in a two-part shell something like the shell of a tiny clam. Some ostracods can give out fluids that cloud water to help hide them from enemies. Others eject fluids to make thread-like ties to hold themselves in certain places, or to use for climbing about.

The copepods, or oar-footed ones, are another group of crustaceans. More water animals feed upon these than on any other one kind of animal known.

Copepod

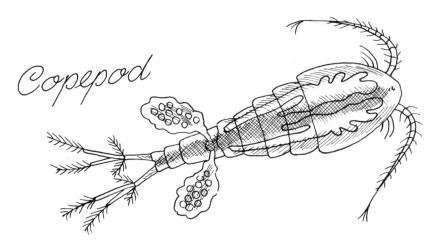

They are very small, but the great numbers of them are unbelievable. They multiply rapidly and this keeps the vast numbers up.

There are two forms of copepods. One kind swims freely about, some even skipping and jumping in the water. When hordes of these lively crustaceans are jumping, it looks as if it were raining on the sea surface.

The second main kind of copepods are parasite crustaceans. This means that they attach themselves to other water creatures by digging into the flesh or scales. They can then get their food by eating at the animals where they are attached. Almost all fish can be hosts to these crustaceans. Small fish, swordfish, sunfish, flying fish, starfish, and even whales are attacked by different sizes and kinds of copepods. Some of the bigger copepods are used in the same manner by other parasite crustaceans that attach themselves to the larger ones.

CONCLUSION

In this book we have glimpsed something of the world of the crustaceans, but we have truly only glimpsed it. It would take a lifetime to really study the numbers and kinds of crustaceans in the world.

Crustaceans from the ocean furnish much food for people and bring millions of dollars each year to those who catch them. The tiny ones that float in teeming numbers furnish food for fish and other creatures of the sea.

It is true that some of the crusty ones are harmful. Some kinds of crabs damage rice fields, eating the tender shoots, knocking the grain over, and burrowing into the dikes until they are weakened. Some kinds of shrimp also cause damage by burrowing.

But, although these damages by crustaceans are problems to be reckoned with, the good that comes from these creatures, taken all together, far outbalances the bad. If all the crusty ones were suddenly to vanish, our world of nature would suffer a stunning blow from which it might never recover.

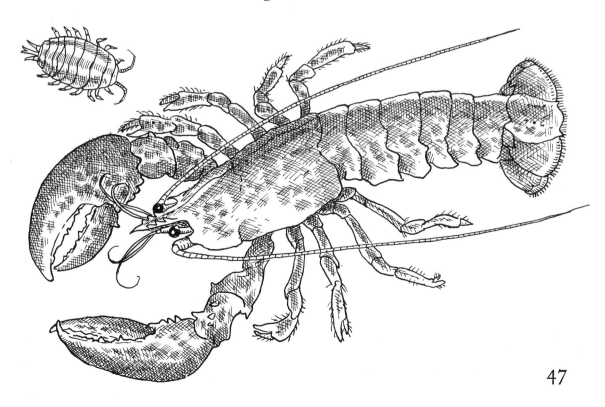